Financial Abuse of the Elderly by Family Members

Have You No Shame?

Sebastian Quinn

The Miserable Three

*A grandmother is to love and adore
she shielded you from winter chill,
Laughed with you in summertime
and hugged you when you were ill,*

*You asked her for financial help
she was ready and so near,
You abused her so very often
requesting more year after year,*

*What a trio of miserable losers
mother, step-father, daughter all,
For we will gather at the OK Corral
where I will surely make you crawl,*

*You may find me at your doorstep
so be cautious you repulsive three,
If not now then in the hereafter
where it will be - just you and me.*

* * *

You know what: Rip me off once, shame on you. Rip me off twice, shame on me. Rip me off three times, you better be prepared for enemy action!

FINANCIAL ABUSE OF THE ELDERLY BY FAMILY MEMBERS – HAVE YOU NO SHAME? I will term this publication as being in the non-fiction/fiction genre.

The underlying facts upon which this book is based are, unfortunately, indeed true and quite accurate. Documentation exists to support the actions of individuals that take place in this book; however, I have changed the names and geographical location for one very important reason to me – my deceased wife's privacy. In this manuscript I'll refer to my wife as 'Katherine.' Further the three members of her family that gutted Katherine (and me) of a substantial sum of money will also be afforded fictitious names – but only to again maintain the privacy for my wife. It is the story that is important – not the identity of the repulsive, disgusting perpetrators.

© 2016 by Sebastian Quinn. All rights reserved. No part of this book may be used or reproduced in any manner whatsoever without written permission of the author or publisher except in the case of very brief quotations embodied in critical articles and reviews.

ISBN-13: 978-1500128579

ISBN -10: 1500128570

Prologue

FINANCIAL ABUSE OF THE ELDERLY BY FAMILY MEMBERS – HAVE YOU NO SHAME?

It is indeed an unfortunate saga all too often encountered today in our society. A society highly debt-ridden, fast-paced, and crowded with non-achievers and those too inept to provide for themselves. It is a story of abject and wretched greed:

- Of the young – and the not so young,
- Of those ill-equipped emotionally and educationally to fend for themselves;
- Of those who lack the tenancy and the drive to be truly self-sufficient and independent;
- Of those too lazy or too lethargic to strive for self-independence or simply;
- Of those too inept to establish their own financial model for success and survival.

Thus they take the life-savings, the limited retirement income of their parents or grandparents, ultimately placing their elder family members in a state of utter financial ruin and heavily burdened by staggering financial debt perhaps even resulting in personal bankruptcy. In any community, especially adult or senior living communities, the stories of family greed and scams is staggering, almost beyond comprehension.

Why is it that those of us now retired often seem to possess far greater financial and property assets and management skills than those in the younger generation; after all we saved and sent our children to college, timely paid the mortgage, tendered the car payments, and still saved for our own retirement. I acknowledge that we are perhaps the last generation receiving partial or full pensions as well as Social Security payments. For the most part we planned for both our current and future needs – stashing money in IRA's, 401k's and 457 Plans as well as traditional savings accounts. I know many individuals today that are in their forties to fifties who will not be entitled to traditional pensions; however, they have saved and contributed on a regular basis in retirement accounts of various kinds often receiving some form of limited match by their employer. These individuals plan for their children's college education, vacations, new homes, and retirement. Unfortunately there seems to be a growing trend for increasing numbers of the next generation where 'planning' is a lost art-form believing they will someday inherit from mother, father, or the grandparents. Some cannot wait for that inheritance and rip-off their parents and grandparents in advance – often leaving the elderly virtually destitute and in a state of utter misery and despair, this is so often true of those now living alone – those widowed or divorced. The following is such a wretched story. Oh how I wish the story I am about to share with you was merely a saga of pure fiction – unfortunately – it is not.

PART ONE - DEATH

Chapter 1

IT IS A LITTLE DIFFICULT for me to state with any degree of certainty when the financial mess actually commenced. Perhaps by simply referring to the circumstance, as a 'financial mess' would indeed be an understatement, maybe 'financial catastrophe and exploitation' might be more apt.

As with so many couples Katherine and I experienced our ups and downs during our years of marriage. To some extent that was true of our finances throughout our twenty-five years together; however, we were solvent and paid our bills timely. Both of us held rather good paying positions of employment and could look forward to defined benefit pensions, as well as Social Security benefits upon retirement.

Sometime in 2002, maybe early 2003 that safety net changed. I simply did not know it at the time. In fact, it would be many years before I would appreciate the extent of our financial devastation. The year 2003 was also the time Katherine and I purchased a new house in a 55+ community. The house was easily affordable for us acquiring our down payment from the profit from the sale of our previous house.

~

There is no doubt in my mind that Katherine was a very intelligent, loving, good and decent lady – perhaps the type of person so easily deceived by unscrupulous children and grandchildren. I still read from time to time the many cards, notes, and letters Katherine wrote me during our many years together. At times there are tears of joy as well as sadness as I read her words

When she died in October of the year 2012, we had journeyed together through life for some twenty-five years - most of those years filled with happiness, joy, and anticipation of the future – thoughts of vacations at the Hotel Hershey in Pennsylvania, of the Samoset Resort or Bar Harbor in Maine, maybe an excursion across country on the American Orient Express. Both Katherine and I had a child by previous marriage – Katherine a daughter and me a son, both married.

Financial Abuse of the Elderly by Family Members Have You No Shame?

Prior to her retirement, Katherine, with a Ph.D. in clinical psychology occupied a senior human resource management position with a regional governmental organization, and I – a lawyer and adjunct professor at the state university.

For many years we seemed to be extremely happy together; Katherine elected to retire quite early in part due to health issues as well as to pursue her various personal passions - quilting, golf, painting, and photography. She excelled at all of these endeavors. Katherine, as with so many employees of our generation, was fortunate – upon retirement she received a significant pension and was entitled to substantial Social Security benefits. Due to her early retirement, benefits under both the pension and Social Security system were reduced significantly, but I remained working fulltime and our overall debt was very limited but for the mortgage and a home equity loan.

Katherine enjoined participating in three ladies' golf leagues, even captain of one, and a local quilting guild. She even worked part-time in a local quilt shop and taught classes in both machine and hand quilting. I believe it is fair to state that Katherine was enjoying life and her many passions to the fullest – we seemed to be enjoying a very nice life together.

Perhaps I should be more specific as to the reasons for Katherine's early retirement. 'Yes,' she wanted to start enjoying new adventures in life – the golf, the quilting, the photography, and the painting. Unfortunately, she had developed at a rather early age COPD, official name 'Chronic Obstructive Pulmonary Disease,' an extremely progressive and debilitating lung disease that over time greatly restricted her breathing ability.

Katherine attempted to remain as physically fit and active as possible in an effort to mitigate the ravages and limitations of the disease. On a regular basis she participated in Yoga, Yoga Rhythmics, Pilates, and Meditation programs, in part to maintain her overall physical fitness, and in part to counter the ever steady progression of her ever-increasing breathing difficulties.

It was about seven years after her retirement that we purchased a new house in a 'fifty-five plus' adult community, again that was the year 2003. It was a large, beautiful house with a gas fireplace, sunroom, whirlpool, gourmet kitchen with granite counter tops and island, hardwood flooring, and

Financial Abuse of the Elderly by Family Members
Have You No Shame?

two-car garage where we housed our two Volvos, an XC90 and a S60 Turbo.

For many years life seemed good, perhaps too good. Or maybe I became complacent, rather naive. In hindsight I appreciate that certain events should have rendered me suspicious, not so much of Katherine herself but of her daughter, Maud, and son-in-law Hector. Perhaps in part I allowed myself to ignore very obvious signs rather than tendering somewhat negative thoughts to Katherine about her daughter and son-in-law. In hindsight, my silence was indeed a very poor decision. I so regret it now.

Perhaps I am moving ahead of myself. I really need to move back in time to about the year 2001. The year 2001 I now consider an important moment in infamy, a watershed.

Chapter 2

TO THE BEST OF MY recollection I became somewhat uneasy in 2001 when Katherine's daughter and son-in-law entered into a contract to buy a house, a rather large house in an upscale community. I had even mentioned to Katherine 'how can they possibly afford that house?' A very clear signal of the forthcoming disaster came a few days before they were to attend settlement on the house. Her daughter Maud asked to borrow $5,000 from me to help pay settlement costs. She promised that the money would be returned to me in a week. To be honest, I made the loan for Katherine, not Maud and Hector. When two weeks had passed and no word from Maud, I became increasing uneasy. I had to ask 'where is the money?' Of course, they were a bit short at that time – short by $5,000. It was some three years later when I received some of the money, about $3,500 as I recall. My guess is that the $3,500 they probably borrowed from someone, maybe even my wife Katherine. Maud and Hector

Financial Abuse of the Elderly by Family Members
Have You No Shame?

quite obviously purchased a house beyond their financial means and ability to pay, that would come to haunt all of us over the ensuing years. Why individuals do that is beyond my comprehension. Do you suppose they are merely stupid, or always believing mom will bail they out of their self-made financial quagmire? From my perspective, it was a bit of both – plus greed, excessive greed!

~

Maud had one daughter, Christine, prior to her marriage to Hector. Together Maud and Hector also had three additional children. Christine was a rather intelligent individual but seemed to lack independence and the ability to indeed accept an appropriate degree of personal responsibility for her actions and expenses – actions that, in turn, affected others. It was always evident that Christine was extremely close to Katherine, her grandmother, probably much more so than her own mother.

It was many years later I would discover that Katherine had in fact been providing significant financial support to Christine for a period of many years. Katherine even paid for some of Christine's dental and medical costs, as well as tuition deposits for Christine's first year at the university. No doubt

Katherine made payments for much more than simply the tuition deposit. Christine even asked Katherine to co-sign her student loans. Apparently neither her mother nor her stepfather was willing to co-sign the documents themselves. Christine didn't survive her initial college year. Soon after departing the college campus she gave birth to the first of her two children. During these years I was unaware of these expenditures and commitments by Katherine. In part, I must blame myself for being naïve and not questioning extremely obvious signs. Katherine was asking me to pay more and more of our monthly expenses even though she was still receiving her pension and Social Security benefits.

Facts discovered later would reveal clearly that Katherine over a period of many years provided significant financial support to Maud, Hector, and Christine. By significant amount I mean an amount well in excess of $100,000. Katherine even paid the daycare fees for Christine's two children; an amount exceeding $1,000 monthly. Evidence revealed in bank and credit card records established without doubt that Maud and Hector continued borrowing monies from Katherine – of course, they never repaid a penny.

Financial Abuse of the Elderly by Family Members
Have You No Shame?

~

Again I must, in part, place some of the blame, the culpability, on me – on my failure to investigate and challenge these actions. Of course, hindsight is simply 'hindsight.'

For now let's move forward to October 2012; a very terrible moment in time.

Chapter 3

DURING THE YEAR 2012 KATHERINE'S COPD seemed to advance quite rapidly. The COPD was also accompanied by ever advancing heart issues. During this year Katherine was hospitalized for extended periods on two distinct occasions due to her COPD that seemed to me to be progressing rapidly. I believe it is important to note that not only was Katherine providing very significant financial support to Christine for her children's day care and other expenses, Katherine was also transporting Christine's two children to and from daycare on a daily basis. It became routine for the two children to stay at our house overnight with Katherine cooking their dinner, bathing them, and putting them to bed – the next morning again transporting them to daycare – with the routine again repeating itself many times a week.

Over a period of time Katherine became extremely exhausted but she felt the need to care for her great grandchildren. To my chagrin and disgust

Financial Abuse of the Elderly by Family Members
Have You No Shame?

I, as an observer, watched as Katherine slowly died. Did Maud, Hector, and Christine care – oh yes indeed they did or would care. When Katherine died – the continuing flow of money to them from Katherine – their 'personal bank' - also died. They cared about that!

For many days prior to Katherine's death, I slept in our front bedroom to allow her to rest more peacefully and without disruption. I would check on her every few hours.

~

In the early morning on Wednesday, October 10, 2012 at 3:00am, I entered into our bedroom to check on Katherine. For many long minutes, before calling '911' I knelt by the bed and held her hand. Katherine had died!

Within minutes of my '911' telephone call, the emergency medical personnel and county police arrived. Although there was no question in my mind, confirmation was made – Katherine had passed-away.

Using Katherine's cellphone that was nestled in its charger on the nightstand next to the bed. I found her brother's telephone number and after returning downstairs called him. Her brother lived on the west coast; he was equally devastated. They had been very close their entire lives. I also called my son who lived in the Midwest. He would fly in the following day to stay with me and assist in all arrangements that needed to be made.

The police were able to contact Maud, Katherine's daughter. Maud and her husband Hector had been separated for some time and I was surprised that shorty they arrived together. When they arrived they immediately dashed upstairs to our bedroom to see Katherine whose body remained on the bed. In hindsight I believe I should have asked the police officer to stop Hector; I had become uncomfortable with him for sometime. I'll explain later. Christine also arrived with her two children and their father who was estranged from Christine. Christine also went upstairs to see her grandmother.

Typically the charger for my cellphone remained on the kitchen counter adjacent to the blender and coffee maker. I inserted Katherine's cell phone in that charger realizing that I would need information contained in it, especially telephone numbers. When her cellphone was fully charged, I placed it on the kitchen island and then placed my cellphone in the charger.

Financial Abuse of the Elderly by Family Members
Have You No Shame?

I contacted our family doctor by telephone; he would execute her death certificate. After Katherine's body was removed and transported to the funeral home, those in the house departed rapidly. Prior to their departure I noticed that Katherine's cellphone was no longer on the kitchen island. I asked Maud, Hector, and Christine if one of them moved it. I even asked Christine to ask her children. What I received was all denials from all – one or more obviously rather disingenuous.

The police officer, an extremely nice and polite individual, remained with me for a while after Katherine's body was transported to the funeral home and her family members had departed. I truly appreciated the comfort he offered me.

Honestly I'm not sure whether I slept that morning or not – my mind remained in a haze – suddenly the house felt 'empty and lonely.'

Later that same morning I would discover additional facts that were truly devastating.

Chapter 4

LATER IN THE MORNING OF her death, I realized that I would need to notify many entities. So many things change upon the death of a spouse: life and health insurance, pension plans, bank accounts, motor vehicle administration, Social Security Benefits, etc. A truly overwhelming and arduous effort especially when one is in a battered emotional state.

~

That entire day I searched for Katherine's cellphone, charger, and purse containing money, checkbook, wallet, car and house keys, credit cards, and other personal items – and I suspect her address book. As with her cellphone and charger, the purse was not to be found. I will note that when my son arrived, he and I continued that exhaustive search – the items have never been located! Quite obviously, those items had been removed by one of the individuals present in the house during the early

Financial Abuse of the Elderly by Family Members
Have You No Shame?

morning hours on the day of her death. Of course, collusion is possible – meaning that we may have been dealing with thieves rather than a solitary thief. My initial reaction was hatred and disgust that family members would steal such items when my wife's death had just occurred a few hours previously. I would indeed learn that I would be dealing with truly ghastly, revolting, and repulsive individuals who clearly did not 'give a damn' about Katherine only their incessant greed for her money, and mine. The replacement keys and change of locks for the Volvo Katherine typically drove cost me almost $900 but I could not take the chance someone might have them and actually steal the XC90. After all, one or more of them just stole her purse, wallet, and cellphone. I was clearly dealing with a disgusting trio of degenerative thieves.

    I transmitted an email to Maud, Hector, and Christine discussing the missing items and advised that if the items were returned, I would drop the matter and not report it to the police. I advised that the items should be placed between the main front door and the screen door. No response from any of the three; items were not returned.

I then contacted the county police and filed a theft report describing the missing items and the individuals that were in the house that day. Maud, Hector, and Christine were all contacted by the police department and questioned about the missing items. Of course, denials were registered by all three. Quite obviously – one or more of them lied to the county police.

While this mess was ongoing, Katherine's funeral arrangements needed to be made. I was a little stressed when Maud, Christine, my son, and I met with the funeral director but my principal concern was to made appropriate arrangements for Katherine. Of course, I paid all of the expenses of Katherine's funeral, not even an offer of any assistance from Maud, Hector or Christine. Was I surprised - No.

With my son's great help I survived as we completed the many details of Katherine's funeral. Katherine's brother and his wife arrived from the west coast. Although he was obviously devastated, he also offered tremendous moral and financial assistance. I refused the financial assistance but was truly grateful for the offer.

Financial Abuse of the Elderly by Family Members
Have You No Shame?

I have noted earlier that among Katherine's many talents was quilting. Our house contained a great many quilts and quilted wall-hangings. One of Katherine's friends and I selected seven beautiful quilts to be displayed during the funeral services. Christine, Katherine's granddaughter, requested that she be given the task of preparing the music to be played at the service. Collectively we selected many songs to be included. The disk was to contain *Danny Boy* by John McDermott, *What a Wonderful World* by Louis Armstrong, *Have I Told You Lately That I love You* by Van Morrison, *If I Should Fall Behind Wait for Me* by Bruce Springsteen, and many others. At the morning of the services the equipment to play the music was ready. When I asked Christine for the tape or disk, she advised that she could not determine how to create it. She never told anyone of this failure – thus we were unable to have Katherine's favorite music at her services. Frankly I was almost beside myself with abject anger but held it to myself for Katherine's sake.

At the memorial service four of us spoke in addition to the minister. Katherine's brother's wife provided an opening prayer. That was followed by a talk by one of Katherine's longtime girlfriends.

Katherine's brother was next; he presented a very warm and comforting talk about his sister, their early years, and the warmth he felt for her. I was next and last; I wanted to make the final summation. At that juncture the minister – who was the minister of Maud's, Katherine's daughter, church advised me that we were running out of the time he had allotted. I told him, 'Send me an extra bill but never, ever tell me to hurry when I am speaking about my wife.' The minister simply shut-up and thereafter he stayed far away from me. Perhaps my chat was lengthy; after all, Katherine and I had been together for twenty-five years. I reminisced about those twenty-five years and the love I continued to feel for her. When finished I leaned over the casket and kissed her goodbye. I had not prepared any notes but I knew it went well when my son and Katherine's brother smiled and gave me the preverbal 'thumbs-up.'

~

My son returned to the Midwest the day following the funeral services and cremation. He had stayed with me for over a week and needed to return to his work. I was very thankful for his assistance and comfort.

Financial Abuse of the Elderly by Family Members
Have You No Shame?

The evening prior to the return to the west coast of Katherine's brother and his wife, I was to join them for dinner at their hotel. It apparently offered a very nice restaurant and was obviously convenient for them as they prepared for the long flight home departing the following afternoon. We decided to invite Maud, Katherine's daughter, to join us. The three of us waited in the hotel lobby for Maud to arrive. To our surprise when she did arrive Hector, her estranged husband, and their three children accompanied Maud. Obviously the concept of a nice quiet dinner had evaporated. Katherine's brother and I huddled and decided to eat at a nearby casual dining restaurant within walking distance. Once we were seated we ordered light fare only. When the food check arrived, Katherine's brother accepted it and paid the entire bill. I left the tip. Hector, Maud's estranged husband who was there with their three children didn't even look up when the bill was presented. To be candid, during the years I had known him, he never offered to pay such a bill. In my opinion, one consistent aspect of Hector was that he seemed to believe the world owed him a living. I will touch more on this issue later in this saga. Thankfully that limited repast ended and I returned to my home.

    I had arranged with Katherine's brother and his wife that I would transport them from their hotel to the airport the following afternoon. I arrived in late morning in order that the three of us could enjoy a last lunch together. We lunched at a local Irish pub that served excellent broiled crab cakes. Naturally we were dining on my turf and I made sure the waitress presented the bill to me. I said simply 'my treat.' Perhaps we were being a bit nasty – we kidded that if Hector was with us he would be hiding under the table when the check arrived. They had both observed Hector's demeanor the previous evening at bill paying time. I doubt that Hector ever in his life offered to pay for lunch or dinner; after all – cheap is indeed cheap! Their plane departed on schedule and I drove home – to a very, very empty house

Financial Abuse of the Elderly by Family Members
Have You No Shame?

PART TWO – FINANCIAL ABUSE

Chapter 5

MAYBE WE SHOULD COMMENCE WITH a discussion as to what is Financial Exploitation of the Elderly? In essence it is the illegal taking, misuse, or concealment of an older individual's funds, property, or assets.

There are essentially two types of Financial Exploitation of the Elderly:

(1) Exploitation by an 'Individual Known to the Victim,' that individual may be a family member, acquaintance, caregiver, or a person acting under a Power-of-Attorney, or a court appointed fiduciary, and

(2) Exploitation by a 'Stranger' including a con artist, an unscrupulous salesperson, contractor, or an individual representing a bogus charity.

Sebastian Quinn

Every year billions of dollars are lost by the financial exploitation of seniors. Although there are myriad forms of financial abuse by strangers, this discussion will address only the financial abuse of seniors by family members.

~

It came be quite sad what we discover when a spouse dies. Maybe I was simply too trusting, or maybe simply naïve. What I discovered following Katherine's death was indeed a total shock; massive indebtedness in both her name and mine in the form of personal loans, credit cards, secret bank accounts, and our bank line-of-credit previously untapped, maxed-out at $120,000 with a significant portion of that total being transferred to or being used to pay the living expenses of her daughter, ex-son-in-law, and granddaughter.

Prior to Katherine's death I was still working full time and commuting a considerable distance by commuter train, thus Katherine typically received the mail daily. Following her death, I started to receive a surprising number of invoices and unpaid notices addressed to either Katherine, me, or to both of us. I was previously unaware of these accounts. Sifting through documents in her quilting office I discovered

Financial Abuse of the Elderly by Family Members
Have You No Shame?

four accounts at a bank other than the one where we maintained our accounts. Two of the bank accounts were in joint names, Katherine and Christine, her granddaughter. A couple of the accounts revealed massive overdraft fees rendering the account balances negative. It is important to note that I was appointed by the court as administrator of Katherine's estate for probate; thus I was afforded access to all accounts in her name or in her name jointly with others. Therefore I was able to receive and review all documents associated with these accounts. It was a huge packet of information. The results were totally shocking to me. Further I started to receive additional unpaid invoices addressed to me at both the home address as well at the post office box I discovered Katherine had rented.

It is difficult to express with any degree of clarity the emotional struggles I was experiencing with Katherine's death and the financial disaster that had befallen to both of us. Perhaps depression would be an understatement.

I believe it is accurate to state that Katherine expended a minimum of $70,000 and perhaps even $90,000 on behalf of her granddaughter – much of that amount through cash transfers from out now maxed-out line-of-credit. Katherine's now ex-son-in-law Hector received thousands of dollars in loans – of course, never repaid. Katherine's daughter Maud also received thousands and thousands of dollars in cash transfers. Further there were outstanding bank loans. In total I estimate based on the records reviewed that Katherine expended approximately $150,000 to $175,000 on behalf of Maud, Hector, and Christine – not one dollar ever repaid. The result was that suddenly I found myself severely in debt on bank loans and credit cards in my name or jointly with Katherine that I did not previously know existed. To indicate the extent of Katherine's desperation to satisfy the insatiable greed of the three lepers, Katherine even resorted to what are typically termed 'pay-day loans' with exorbitant and outrageous interest rates. See Chapter 13 for a comprehension discussion of 'Payday Loans.'

~

Katherine had dug herself into a very deep hole from which she could not extricate herself. Had she lived the only logical solution would have been the filing of a petition for bankruptcy on her behalf.

My personal situation had also become rather precarious since Katherine had executed many of these bank loans and transactions in my name alone.

Financial Abuse of the Elderly by Family Members
Have You No Shame?

Fortunately I had engaged a very good lawyer for assistance. We would battle for two years – but we always prevailed!

To afford you some idea of the disgusting manner in which these financial transactions were made, I offer a few examples:

- Katherine for the last two years of her life paid approximately $1,150 monthly for the child-care for Christine's two children. This is true even though during the final year of Katherine's life, Christine as a registered nurse was earning in excess of $50,000 annually. In addition to the payment for child-care, Katherine would transport the two children to and from day-care. No repayment ever made by Christine for these expenses and no assistance from Maud or Hector.

- One time when Katherine was unable to retrieve Christine's children from daycare due to a medical appointment, Katherine paid Maud (Christine's mother and the children's grandmother) $70 to retrieve the children from daycare. What a disgusting person is Maud.

- Christine would periodically transmit to Katherine a list of her near term expenses implying of course that Katherine would provide the necessary funds. One such email included; dental expenses (removal of wisdom teeth), vehicle registration fee, hairdresser, apartment monthly rental, eye examination and glasses, dance lessons for children, bank loans (some checks drafted on an account establish in my name), Sallie Mae (student loans), monthly cellphone fees, and food. No repayment ever made by Christine for these expenses.

- Christine routinely charged gasoline and automobile expenses to our gasoline credit card. Over a period of a year the amount exceeded $2,000. No repayment ever made by Christine for these expenses.

Financial Abuse of the Elderly by Family Members
Have You No Shame?

- Christine signed Katherine's signature on a check to pay a photographer's bill – for photographs of her children.

- Christie asked Katherine to co-sign her student loans for the university nursing school when her mother, Maud, and stepfather, Hector, apparently either refused or ignored such a request by Christine for assistance. Naturally, Christine defaulted on these loans. I know this for a fact because the banks extending the loans sought repayment from Katherine. At that juncture, I notified the institutions that Katherine had died and provided a copy of her Death Certificate – thus no repayment. Although I do not know, I suspect Christine never repaid the loans and remains in default.

- In addition to the thousands of dollars paid directly from Katherine to Maud via checks on our line-of-credit, Maud requested that Katherine pay the fees for Maud's son to attend a summer camp. No repayment ever made by Maud for these expenses.

- Maud requested that Katherine provide funding for cleaning services for Maud's house.

- Hector received thousands of dollars paid directly from Katherine to Hector via a check on our line-of-credit (check even identified as a 'loan'). No repayment ever made by Hector. He even ignored a demand for repayment by my lawyer and myself when this matter was discovered.

- Hector transmitted an email to Katherine advising her of his bank account numbers at two banks in order for her to transfer money to him. No repayment ever made by Hector.

- Hector received thousands of dollars from Katherine through bank account transfers.

Financial Abuse of the Elderly by Family Members
Have You No Shame?

As you might imagine, the costs for me to attempt to straighten-out this financial quagmire were quite significant. Fortunately, as stated previously, I had engaged an extremely competent attorney who was quite fair in affording me and the issues the necessary time as well as being fair in billing for his services – services that were extensive and for a protracted period of time – all as a consequence of the actions of Maud, Hector, and Christine.

After a period of time and resolving some demands by creditors for payment I decided to seek information from Christine as to why she sought so much money from her grandmother Katherine. I transmitted to her an email suggesting that we meet at a neutral site to discuss the issues. What I received in return was a visit by the county police extending to me a notice for me to appear in county court if I wished to contest a request for a protective order filed by Christine against me. As a practical matter I suspect the filing by Christine was at the behest of her mother Maud who seemed to direct Christine's actions even though Christine was in her early to mid-twenties at that time. Perhaps it is the time to mention that, in my opinion, Maud was one of the most unsuccessful, and least equipped individuals to succeed I have ever met. Success was not within her grasp – it was simply beyond her comprehension.

At the court hearing concerning the requested protective order, Christine's argument was that she was fearful because I had stated that by the repeated incessant requests for money she had, in part, been the cause of her grandmother's death due to the constant extreme stress that exacerbated Katherine's already precarious health due to advanced COPD and heart related matters. That being the sole basis for her request for the protective order, the court denied her request as 'having no basis for relief.' I have not further attempted to contact Christine – useless individual and an utter waste of time.

Perhaps from my perspective I refer to Maud, Hector, and Christine as merely a perverted trio of 'blood sucking money seekers.' Indeed, the term seems to fit.

Once the unfortunate details of the financial mess were evident, the next step was to develop and coordinate with my lawyer a plan of action – to establish a defense to the myriad of creditors 'knocking on the door' for payment.

Chapter 6

THE INITIAL BATTLE WITH SOME of the creditors was successful. Some of the bank loans executed by Katherine on behalf of Christine were in Katherine's name alone. To counter the demands of these institutions, two things were necessary. I applied to the court to be appointed as Personal Representative of Katherine's estate. Katherine died intestate, meaning without an executed Will. We often discussed executing Joint Wills; it simply never happened. One of my duties as the court appointed Personal Representative of Katherine's estate was to compile an inventory of Katherine's personal assets. Under the law, such assets did not include jointly held property or specifically property held as 'tenants by the entireties' - property owned by husband and wife. As a practical matter, almost all of our property, real and personal, was titled jointly. Thus Katherine's estate was classified as a small estate by the court that had reviewed and approved property listing. In a small estate, certain property to a certain limit is shielded from creditors. Many of the bank and finance loans in Katherine's name alone were thus protected from the reach of creditors. That was the easy part.

~

The true battles commenced with the banks and various creditors where loans and accounts had been created in either my name alone or jointly with Katherine.

You might ask, 'how was a loan originated in my name without my knowledge?' The answer: 'Easy.' Prior to 2012 banks, even those nationally known, lacked any meaningful investigation as to the authentication of signatures on loan or credit documentation. Unfortunately my wife, who was a very good and decent lady bowing to extreme pressure from her family members executed loan documents in my name and forged my signature. Again I admit being naïve and not accepting responsibility to examine and assess my own financial affairs on a regular basis. Had I done so, a significant portion of the difficulties could have been averted. Hindsight is indeed wonderful, but except as a learning tool – useless in these matters.

Financial Abuse of the Elderly by Family Members
Have You No Shame?

What actually ensued was a very protracted and expensive effort to resolve these issues. A substantial amount of time and legal fees were required. I do consider myself fortunate in selecting a knowledgeable and responsible lawyer. Although I am a lawyer, now retired, I adhere to the old adage, somewhat revised, ' A person, even if he or she be a lawyer, who represents himself or herself, has a fool for a client.' Clearly I was not in an emotional estate to handle the legal issues.

In a couple of instances, especially those concerning bank and finance company loans, we came quite close to battles in court. My lawyer and I persevered through sheer tenacity and the belief that defeat, even through settlement, was unacceptable. Perhaps I am merely a 'hard-ass' but agreeing to make payment for something I did not originate was against my emotional grain. It does necessitate a substantial and protracted effort but we should not cave to unwarranted demands.

~

Is That Really My Signature?

One issue that was quite important was the authentication or validation of what purported to be my signature. We were able to establish that certain signatures on documents were not in fact mine, even though my name was on the document. In one in case a finance company loaned my wife funds based on my 'purported signature' as contained on an online application. Our position to the finance company was simple, 'be prepared to prove in court that the electronic signature is in fact mime.' That finance company finally caved and we received a official letter withdrawing its claim.

~

BAD CREDIT REPORTS

Oftentimes when a bank or finance company is unable to obtain repayment it will file with the appropriate agency a 'bad credit' rating for the person purportedly responsible for such repayment. That was true in my own situation. Although two finance companies threatened the filing of bad credit, one company actually did so. Thus my credit report reflected this filing. This became one of the more difficult issues to resolve. From my perspective we easily established that the signature of the loan document was, in fact, not my signature and in fact resembled that of my wife. We advised

Financial Abuse of the Elderly by Family Members
Have You No Shame?

that finance company that we would be filing an official complaint with the State Attorney General as well as other appropriate agencies. A stalemate seemed to prevail until the legal counsel for that finance company became involved directly. Following a very thorough review and analysis of the signature on the document compared with various versions of my original signature, the legal counsel for the finance company concurred with us, 'the signature on the loan document was, in fact, not mine.' The finance company notified the credit reporting agencies that there was no basis for its initial filing and thus requested the bad credit notification be withdrawn. It was a long, arduous battle – but worth it to me.

~

JOINT LINE-OF-CREDIT

When Katherine and I applied for a mortgage for our new home in a 55+ community we were approved. The bank also offered us a pre-approved line-of-credit in the amount of $120,000. Perhaps without considering potential consequences we accepted. That line-of-credit remained unused for years. One day I was discussing with the bank a possible reduction in the mortgage interest rate, and the issue of the line-of-credit arose. I discovered that the line-of-credit was virtually 'maxed-out.' Again you might ask, 'who could you not know?' Well again we might call it stupidity or naivety. I allowed myself to be gullible – simply trusting too much. Should I have known? In all probability the answer is 'yes.' I also blame the bank – I'll explain.

As I understand the then procedure, any daily line-of-credit withdrawals of $3,000 or less did not necessitate a review or notification of all potentially responsible parties. Thus my wife was able to execute successive withdrawals of $3,000. In addition to the many cash withdrawals, Katherine issued many line-of-credit checks for thousands of dollars to her daughter, Maud, and her then son-in-law, Hector. The line-of-credit was 'maxed-out' at $120,000. I note that many of the $3,000 cash withdrawals were used to pay the expenses of Katherine's granddaughter Christine for apartment rent, food, medical and dental expenses, hairdresser, and childcare. Responsible parents, certainly not Maud or Hector, would have assisted Christine themselves and not allowed these obscene amounts to be paid by Katherine, Christine's grandmother

Financial Abuse of the Elderly by Family Members
Have You No Shame?

who lived on a fixed, limited income. Of course, none of these funds were ever repaid.

~

STUDENT LOANS

After Katherine's death I started to receive student loan statements addressed to her from two banks. Such statements indicated tens of thousands of dollars in late or unpaid student loans. These student loans were for the benefit of Christine in paying her college tuition costs. Christine was the originator of the loans but due to her then lack of income the banks required a co-signer. Obviously both Maud and Hector made themselves unavailable as co-signers - typical of them and once again demonstrating their utter deficiency with respect to their parental responsibility. Fortunately this issue was rather easily resolved by the substantiation of Katherine's death and lack of available estate assets. But still – Katherine should never have been the co-signer; it should have been Maud and Hector.

Perhaps losers such as Maud, Hector, and Christine should realize they to will be a senior someday; perhaps with good fortune – they too will be financial abused by their offspring. There is always hope for retribution!

Chapter 7

ALTHOUGH NOT APPLICABLE TO MY personal situation, I would be remiss if I did not mention the potential horrors of Powers-of-Attorney. You might ask, 'what is a Power-of Attorney?'

In essence a Power-of-Attorney is a written and signed authorization to represent another or act on another's behalf in business or personal matters. The person authorizing the other to act is the principal or grantor of the power. The one authorized to act is the agent or grantee of the power. With respect to Powers-of-Attorney, I have three initial comments: BEWARE, BEWARE and BEWARE.

Powers-of-Attorney will allow the grantee of the power to use, control, and – deplete the financial assets of the grantor. In affect a legal theft. A Power-of-Attorney is indeed often referred to as a 'License to Steal.'

Financial Abuse of the Elderly by Family Members Have You No Shame?

There are two basic types of Powers-of-Attorney: (1) a Durable Power-of-Attorney, and a Springing Power-of-Attorney.

A <u>Durable Power-of-Attorney</u> occurs when a Principal designates another as the Agent or Grantee and possessing unrestricted power to handle the Grantor's finances unless otherwise specified in the document.

A <u>Springing Power-of-Attorney</u> occurs when the Agent's authority or power springs into effect upon the happening of a certain event such as when the Grantor becomes incapacitated.

The Agent or the Grantee under a Power-of-Attorney has certain responsibilities such as: (1) to act in accordance with the Grantor wishes; (2) to act with care, competence, and diligence for the best interests of the Grantor; (3) to only act within the scope of the authority granted; (4) to maintain a detailed record of all receipts, disbursements, and transactions made on behalf of the Grantor; and (5) to avoid any conflict-of-interest that impairs the Agent's or Grantee's ability to act impartially in the Grantor's best interest.

From a reasonable safety perspective it may be beneficial on the part of the Grantor (1) to only execute a Power-of-Attorney if needed or there is reason to believe it will be needed, (2) to review the financial competency of the proposed Grantee, (3) to be specific as to what actions will be allowed and specifically what is not allowed, and (4) to include third-party monitoring.

Chapter 8

EARLIER IN THIS DOCUMENT I discussed the theft of Katherine's Purse containing her Wallet, Credit Cards, Cash, Telephone and Note Book, Car and House Keys – her Cellphone and Phone Charger, etc.

The County Police Department was notified immediately and a theft report filed of this matter. Since the only individuals that entered our bedroom on the second floor of the house – in addition to the emergency personnel, police and me – were Maud, Hector, and Christine; obviously one or more of the very 'Disgusting Three' was/were the perpetrator(s) of the theft. The County Police contacted each of the three – all denied the removal of Katherine's purse, cellphone, etc. Although her cellphone was removed from the kitchen island, the cellphone charger was, in fact, removed from the bedside table in our bedroom.

In an effort to track the current location of Katherine's cellphone, I inquired at the cellphone service provider store as to whether the current location of the phone could be ascertained. I advised that the County Police would be informed. To be candid, the cellphone service provider personnel were not very cooperative demanding a copy of Katherine's Death Certificate prior to cancelling her multiannual subscription. The relevant information I received was that to trace the present location of the cellphone an imbedded special chip was necessary. According to the provider's records, Katherine's cellphone did not contain such a chip. Too bad – if the cellphone had contained such a chip, Maud, Hector, and/or Christine may have been a resident in jail before sunset.

This theft resulted in many consequences: the necessity of having the dealership change the automatic keys and codes to the vehicle Katherine typically drove, all locks to the house, cancellation of bank credit and debit cards, and notification to the state's Department of Motor Vehicles. The death of a spouse requires a considerable quantity of paperwork; the theft of her valuables by family members exacerbates greatly these issues.

Financial Abuse of the Elderly by Family Members
Have You No Shame?

Should you ever find yourself in a situation comparable to mine, I recommend that you contact the Police Department of the city or county in which you live. This is not the time to suffer in silence and allow the perpetrators to escape liability. If you are embarrassed that this happened to you, put the embarrassment on the far back burner and do something. The sooner you contact the police, the greater the possibility of retrieval of the items and, quick punishment for the thieves. Unfortunately, according to police statistics only a very small percentage of such victims ever file such a theft report with the police. Seeking to maintain family harmony, even if it actually exists, is not the road to satisfaction. After all – a thief is indeed a thief. If is occurred once, it may indeed, and in all probability will, happen again.

I urge you to contemplate the 'chip.' Contact your service provider and determine whether or not your cellphone and that of your spouse contains such a chip. If not – consider having it added. The potential benefit could be immeasurable.

Chapter 9

BEFORE YOU EXPERIENCE THE DEATH of a spouse you should consider legal ownership of property. Typically the house, considered 'real property,' will not present a problem. In many, but not all, jurisdictions the property will automatically be titled in the case of married couples as 'Tenants by the Entireties.' Many others, however, use the 'Community Property Doctrine.' Be sure to known and understand the form of ownership in your state. To a significant extent, the same will be true of what is termed 'personal property' – typically 'personal property' is all property not considered 'real property.'

For example in a 'Tenants by the Entireties' jurisdiction, ownership in the property will vest automatically in the surviving spouse. Thus, should your wife or husband die, you as the surviving spouse will become 100% owner of the property. I would suggest that a joint-will be prepared by a

Financial Abuse of the Elderly by Family Members
Have You No Shame?

competent attorney – do not simply download a form from the Internet. This issue is too important. There may be unfortunate times when a relative, an unscrupulous relative of your spouse will attempt to contend that he or she is entitled to certain property of your deceased spouse. The typical answer is 'No.' The exception may be what is often termed 'pre-owned property' – property owned by a spouse prior to your marriage. Laws differ and should be reviewed by your attorney.

There are times when a child or sibling of a deceased spouse will attempt to take property of the deceased spouse. I offer a very horrible example, addressed previously, of what occurred at my wife's memorial service. My wife was a lady of many talents, one of which was quilting. For her memorial service seven quilts that were in our home were selected for display at the service. They were some of her most beautiful quilts. A memorial service for a spouse is difficult in itself and we do not pay attention to everything. At the conclusion of the service, her daughter Maud removed and took home the seven quilts and refused to return them. But for the audacity of her thievery, I probably would have offered her some of Katherine's quilts. That thievery coupled with the thief of Katherine's purse, cellphone, etc. during the morning of her death resulted in a de-facto state-of-war with Maud, Maud's ex-husband Hector, and her granddaughter Christine. In fact the thief by Maud of the seven quilts convinced me that she was indeed one of the perpetrators that stole Katherine's purse, cellphone, etc.

Fortunately both vehicles were titled in both of our names. Almost immediately after Katherine's death, Maud requested to borrow 'her mother's car.' I saw the import of that statement immediately and informed Maud that both vehicles were titled in our names, Katherine and mine. With some degree of trepidation I loaned her the vehicle for a day or so. Almost immediately one of Katherine's relatives told Maud to return the vehicle.

My advice – be careful – do not relinquish possess of any items that will not be transferred to a relative – you may never see it again. It has been years since Katherine's death – I have never again see those seven quilts.

You may not be comfortable denying the requests by relatives of your deceased spouse for

Financial Abuse of the Elderly by Family Members
Have You No Shame?

specific property, but you need to be quite strong. Do not comply with such requests too quickly. It is the time for logic, not emotions – difficult as that may be.

Chapter 10

I WAS SO DISGUSTED WITH the thievery of Katherine's items and the belligerent attitude of Maud, Hector, and Christine that I filed an official complaint with the Office of the State Attorney General.

The document submitted to the Attorney General, and later the County State's Attorney Office, presented a detailed discussion of the financial abuse perpetrated by Maud, Hector, and Christine on Katherine and indirectly on me. The submission included a significant number of documents appended and supporting the discussion. Such document included requests for money, bank account transfers, payments by Katherine of Christine's financial obligations, as well as those of Maud and Hector. The amount associated with the financial abuse totaled a minimum of $150,000, much of it as checks written on our joint line-of-credit and loans originated in Katherine's name as well as mine –my signature having been forged by Katherine.

Financial Abuse of the Elderly by Family Members
Have You No Shame?

The Office of the Attorney General for the state declined to file a complaint against Maud. Hector, and Christine and suggested the matter be filed with the Office of the County State's Attorney. It in turn declined to charge criminally the three perpetrators. My belief is that both offices are today inundated with such complaints; after all, financial abuse of the elderly is big business. For all practical purposes, due to these sheer volumes we may be relegated to self-help.

Chapter 11

FROM MY PERSPECTIVE, RACE WAS a significant issue in this disgusting scenario. My negative feelings for Katherine in creating such major debt for her as well as for me have been ameliorated to a significant degree by Katherine's history. Katherine and I were a duo in a mixed-race marriage. I am White or Caucasian of English and Irish ancestry. Katherine was African-American or as she preferred 'Of Color.' One important aspect of Katherine's history is that she was born and raised in the South – in the South during the period of legislated segregation. Being a Caucasian it is difficult for me to comprehend the adverse emotional impact of being a minority in a segregated environment. The treatment associated with schools, restaurants, transportation, etc. must have been abhorrent to a human being. Fortunately for Katherine, she departed the South for college on the West Coast.

Financial Abuse of the Elderly by Family Members
Have You No Shame?

Although Katherine left the South I have no doubt the vestiges of segregation never fully left her, but stayed with her for the remainder of her life.

I have always believed that Katherine's over extension of financial support for her granddaughter was predicated on the years of incessant segregation Katherine had endured in her pre-college years. I suspect that Maud and Hector in particular used these feelings to exploit Katherine and eradicate her of her money. Certainly discrimination remains today but legislated segregation was most definitely a truly repulsive world in which to exist.

Katherine and I were together for twenty-five years. In the early years we were the objects of a few stares but over the ensuing years one witnessed more and more mixed-race couples. I will note we did not live in the deep South. I have no idea as to what life as a mixed-race couple there would be even today.

In my own mind I believe that much of Katherine's motivation to assist Christine was based on the desire to insure that Christine enjoyed a better and more pleasant childhood that Katherine had experienced under the insidious laws associated with segregation. Unfortunately Maud, Hector, and Christine simply took advantage of Katherine's generosity with Christine even sending Katherine emails of monies she would be needing for rent, child daycare, medical and dental expenses, hairdresser, food, and car maintenance. Of course, neither Maud nor Hector ever accepted any responsibility as a parent for Christine's expenses – they merely abdicated all responsibility – both parental and moral. What a pair of deadbeats in human form. Some individuals should never be parents. Maybe in some manner Katherine was simply too good of a person, especially as a grandmother in an effort to protect and insure success for her granddaughter.

Chapter 12

THERE IS NO DOUBT THAT stress was an important element leading to the death of my wife. I do not dismiss her COPD and heart issues; however, the degree of stress under which she lived due to the constant requests for money from Maud, Hector, and Christine coupled with harassing telephone calls and demands for payment by creditors pushed her beyond human endurance.

Many studies have identified stress as a significant factor in the premature death of an individual. When one combines extreme stress with advanced Chronic Obstructive Pulmonary Disease and Heart Disease, it is indeed a combination for disaster – for death. Katherine's medical issues alone were very significant and advancing; the combination with the continuing stress caused by the incessant demands for more and more money was a combination for disaster – in my opinion Katherine's death. Katherine's death certificate stated the cause of death as Advanced COPD and Heart Failure. To me, it could more appropriately state: 'Extreme Stress resulting from Excessive Demands for Money from Unscrupulous and Abusive Relatives.'

There were many times when I noticed Katherine sitting on the sofa in the living room – not really talking to me or watching television or working on a quilt block. She just seemed to be staring into space. I would ask if everything was okay; she wound reply 'yes.' I felt something was wrong but I didn't want to probe too much. Again being naïve, I thought perhaps she was concerned about her medical issues. In hindsight, I should have probed more deeply! I will always fault myself for not doing so.

I became aware of the fact that Katherine was seeing a psychiatrist on a somewhat regular basis. Once again, I did not probe believing the discussions were related to her medical condition. After Katherine's death and my discovery of the extent of the financial mess surrounding her, I attempted to discuss the matter with her psychiatrist but was advised that any disclosure of those discussions would be a violation of the doctor-

Financial Abuse of the Elderly by Family Members
Have You No Shame?

patient relationship. This was a barrier I was not able to breach. In hindsight I have little doubt that much of the discussions centered on the evolving financial fiasco surrounding Katherine.

Chapter 13

THE SCOURGE OF 'PAYDAY LOANS.'

A payday loan is a short-term loan, generally for $500 or less – repayment is typically due on your next payday.

Payday loans generally have three common features:

- The loans are for small amounts of money.
- The loans typically come due your next payday.
- You must give lenders access to your checking account or write a check for the full balance in advance - the lender has an option of depositing when the loan comes due.

There are quite often other significant loan

Financial Abuse of the Elderly by Family Members
Have You No Shame?

features. For example, payday loans are typically structured to be paid-off in one lump-sum payment, but interest-only payments – "renewals" or "rollovers" – are not unusual. In some situations, payday loans may be structured so that they are repayable in installments over a longer period of time.

Lenders can deliver the funds by: providing cash or a check, loading the funds onto a prepaid debit card, or electronically depositing the money into your checking account.

The cost to the borrower of the loan (the finance charge) may range from $10 to $30 for every $100 received. A typical two-week payday loan with a $15 per $100 fee equates to an annual percentage rate (APR) of almost 400%. By comparison, APRs on credit cards typically range from about 12 percent to 30 percent.

Not all states allow payday loans - others place significant restrictions on them. Let's examine a few jurisdictions:

California State Information
Legal Status: Legal
Citation: Cal. Fin. Code §§ 23000 to 23106
Loan Terms: Maximum Loan Amount: $300
Loan Term: Max: 31 days
Maximum Finance Rate and Fees: 15% of check
Finance Charge for 14-day $100 loan: $17.65
  APR for 14-day $100 loan: 459%

Florida State Information
Legal Status: Legal
Citation: Fl. Stat. Ann. §§ 560.402 et seq.;
  Rules 69V-560.707, 69V-560.901-912
Loan Terms: Maximum Loan Amount: $500
Loan Term: 7-31 days
Maximum Finance Rate and Fees: 10% of check +
  verification fee not to exceed $5
Finance Charge for 14-day $100 loan: $16.11
APR for 14-day $100 loan: 419%

Illinois State Information
Legal Status: Legal
Citation: Ill. Comp. Stat. §§ 122/1-1 et seq.
Loan Terms: Maximum Loan Amount: lesser of

Financial Abuse of the Elderly by Family Members
Have You No Shame?

$1000 or 25% gross monthly income
Loan Term: 13-45 days
Maximum Finance Rate and Fees: $15.50 per $100
Finance Charge for 14-day $100 loan: $15.50
APR for 14-day $100 loan: 403%

Maryland State Information
Legal Status: Prohibited
Citation: Consumer loan act applies.
> Md. Code Com. Law § 12-101 et seq.

Small Loan Rate Cap: 2.75% per month; 33%
> per year.

Pennsylvania State Information
Legal Status: Prohibited
Citation: Check cashers are specifically prohibited
> from making payday loans. 63 Penn Stat.
> Ann. § 2325. Otherwise, Consumer Discount
> Company Act applies. 7 Pa. Cons. Stat. §§
> 6201 et seq.

Small Loan Rate Cap: $9.50 per $100 per year
> interest, plus service charge of $1.50 per
> $100 per year.

Texas State Information

Legal Status: Legal

Citation: 7 Tex. Admin. Code § 83.604; 4 Tex. Fin. Code §§ 342.251 et seq. and §§ 342.601 et seq.

Loan Terms: Maximum Loan Amount: Not specified

Loan Term: 7-31 days

Maximum Finance Rate and Fees: May not exceed rates authorized in Tex. Fin. Code §§ 342.251 - 342.259. 7 Tex. Admin Code § 83.604 provides a chart stating that maximum APRs for payday loans range from 83.43% for a 30- day, $350 loan to 569.92% for a 7-day, $100 loan.

Finance Charge for 14-day $100 loan: $11.87

APR for 14-day $100 loan: 309.47%

Source: 'Payday Loan Consumer Information (See the following for all jurisdictions) http://www.paydayloaninfo.org/state-information

~

A recent article in *ABC News, Savanna Kim, May 20, 2016,* discussed a Missouri man who paid

Financial Abuse of the Elderly by Family Members
Have You No Shame?

$50,000 in interest after receiving $2,500 in Payday Loans.

http://abcnews.go.com/Business/missouri-man-paid-50000-interest-taking-2500-payday/story?id=39253982

In another article posted *January 2009 in Consumer Reports Magazine* issue: February 2009 An Individual ended up paying $600 in fees on a $400 payday loan. The individual took out a $400 loan from an online lender, which charged her an additional $120 to borrow the money for just 16 days. That's comparable to an annual interest rate of 684 percent. When the individual did not have the full $520 to repay at the end of the 16 days, the person 'rolled over' the loan for another $120 in fees. Ultimately the borrower had rolled over the loan five times and paid $600 in fees on the $400 loan.
http://www.consumerreports.org/cro/aboutus/mission/viewpoint/small-loan-big-problems/overview/small-loan-big-trouble-ov.

Sebastian Quinn

Consumer Financial Protection Bureau's Proposed Rules Concerning Payday Loans

The payday loan industry as it exists today could soon be a thing of the past – many changes could be forthcoming.

Recently federal regulators issued proposed rules that would drastically restrict access to payday loans and restrict destructive practices carried out by lenders of such loans.

Borrowers of payday loans receive quick access to cash, but there is a significant downside, extremely high interest rates and short repayment periods. Many borrowers who subject themselves to payday loans cannot afford to pay them back in a timely manner – thus they greatly overextend themselves resulting in executing new loans resulting in a vicious cycle of more and more loans. Result – the borrowers find themselves stuck in an endless cycle of debt.

Under the proposed rules, the Consumer Financial Protection Bureau (CFPB) would require lenders to take into consideration a borrower's ability to repay the loan by examining the borrowers' income, borrowing history and

Financial Abuse of the Elderly by Family Members Have You No Shame?

current and ongoing financial obligations. The rules would also put a cap on the number of loans that can be made in quick succession and restrict the ways in which lenders can seek repayment.

The consequence of payday loans to many borrowers seeking an infusion of short-term cash is that they are burdened with additional debt that is beyond their ability to repay.

Although many states have rules and interest rate caps designed to protect consumers, many do not. Interest rates typically approach 390% and someone who takes out a payday loan can expect to pay what is termed a median fee or finance fee of $15 for every $100 borrowed. Statistically eighty percent of all payday loans are rolled over or renewed within two weeks.

Payday loans are a $38.5 billion industry - the underlying premise being that borrowers will not be able to timely payoff the outstanding loan balance and need to resort to a further succession of payday loans. The proposed rules would restrict the number of times someone can take out or refinance payday loans within a certain amount of time.

Lenders are also often granted access to a

borrower's bank account and can make repeated attempts to withdraw funds, triggering significant bank fees. Under the proposed rules, lenders would have to give written notice before attempting to collect a loan payment, and could try only twice before having to get new authorization from the borrower.

It will now solicit comments on the proposed rules through September 14, 2016 before final regulations are issued.

Chapter 14

THERE ARE INDEED MANY OTHER types of financial scams perpetrated on seniors citizens other than by family and friends. You should become aware of these:

- **GREEN DOT CARDS**: Is a Prepaid Card purchased at various types of retail stores. A stranger – a scammer, notifies you that you have won a specific prize; however, in order to receive the prize you must place a designated sum of money on the card. Subsequent to the money being loaded on the card you are then asked for the specific card number; thereafter, of course, the perpetrator withdraws the money. Goodbye money – it is now long done.

- **IRS TAX SCAMS**: A telephone call is received from someone claiming to be an IRS agent. The caller states that there is an outstanding arrest warrant filed against you for back income taxes. The victim is then advised that the arrest warrant can be withdrawn by payment of amount of the alleged back taxes via credit/debit card or green dot card. Of course, the money on the card is gone – there were no back taxes due.

- **CHARITY SCAMS**: The victim receives a telephone call thanking him or her for a previous pledge – perhaps you do not recall that alleged previous donation – there probably never was one. The victim is then asked for an additional pledge by cash or via wire transfer.

- **TELEMARKETING SCAMS**: A telephone call is received employing high-pressure tactics for a wide range of causes such as: Fraudulent Investments, Foreign and

Financial Abuse of the Elderly by Family Members
Have You No Shame?

Domestic Travel Packages, Sweepstake and Lotteries, and Home Improvement Schemes. It is then that the telemarketer requests your personal information for verification. Definitely, this is the time to hang-up quickly!

- **COUNTERFEIT PRESCRIPTION DRUG SCAMS**: Such scams are most typically operated via the Internet where seniors seek to purchase specialized medications at greatly reduced prices. Often the medications are unsafe or lack the actual drug itself.

- **CREDIT CARD SCAMS**: The victim is notified by telephone and advised that one or more of his/her credit cards have been compromised. The victim is then advised that in order to receive assistance to clear the card the credit cards must either be relinquished or that personal information must be revealed.

- **ONLINE ROMANCE SCAM**: An individual with whom you have been chatting via a dating website requests you leave that website in order that the two of you may further communicate via personal email.

   Often that individual expresses almost immediate feelings of love. He claims to be a citizen of the United States and is working overseas. He notifies that he would like to visit you but is unable due to an unforeseen event and request that you wire him some money.

   Well – money is gone and so is your new friend.

Chapter 15

THE POSSIBILIY OF COLLUSION BETWEEN family members and caregivers or others may exist. Collusion is essentially secret or illegal cooperation or conspiracy, especially in order to cheat or deceive others.

It is a possibility that a family member may enter into an agreement with a caregiver to spy on the elderly family member in an effort to obtain vital financial information or the location of valuable personal property.

For our purposes, a Caregiver is defined as a person who gives help, assistance, and protection to someone such an elderly individual who requires assistance in daily activities such as dressing, bathing, cooking, cleaning, etc. At times a Caregiver may also be involved with assisting the elderly individual in the payment of expenses and bank accounts. With respect to financial assistance, I would recommend that this activity not occur. Of course, if the Caregiver is also a family member assistance with financial matters may be necessary; however, there should be a trusted individual that overseas such actions by the Caregiver.

Assistance by a family member of an elderly individual's finances is obviously fraught with potential troubles for it is often the family member that is the thief – often disguised as the helpful, loyal, loving daughter, son, grandchild, etc. One activity that may help in this matter is having a lawyer, accountant, financial advisor, etc. oversea and review all financial aspects of transactions initiated or implemented by the Caregiver. I highly recommend that a competent individual review all transactions initiated by a Caregiver above a designated dollar limit. Further, an annual accounting of all expenses and receipts should be required and reviewed by an independent third party.

I would suggest that a Caregiver never be authorized via a Power of Attorney to make major financial decisions. The exception might be the issuance of a Power of Attorney to a trusted family member – obviously with a follow-on independent review.

Financial Abuse of the Elderly by Family Members
Have You No Shame?

Perhaps it goes without saying but a criminal background check is absolutely essential as well as a comprehensive discussion with the Caregiver's references. Always, but always, require the criminal background check and references. Better safe than sorry. As part of the employment process a personal interview should be conducted. This not only allows you to ask all relevant questions but also to observe the Caregiver's demeanor, appearance, deportment, and attitude.

I would also recommend that the Caregiver selected be both Bonded and Licensed.

It is important that someone watches for signs of abuse, neglect, and exploitation, and reports any suspicious activity to the agency and state authorities. This is not the time for second chances; the finances and health of the elderly family member is at stake.

Chapter 16

IF YOU OR A FAMILY member are the subject of financial abuse by a family member, friend, caregiver, or stranger, seek help immediately.

The following are organizations that offer you assistance in these matters:

The Senior Citizen Liaison of your Local City or County Police Department

~

National Committee for the Prevention of Elder Abuse, 1730 Rhode Island Avenue, N.W., Washington, D.C.

~

Financial Abuse of the Elderly by Family Members
Have You No Shame?

The **American Psychological Association** offers publications, videos, and statistics as well as help with financial elder abuse. See,

http://www.apa.org/pi/prevent-violence/resources/elder-abuse.aspx

~

The National Council on Aging (NCOA): A nonprofit service and advocacy organization that offers resources for older adults and caregivers. See,

https://www.ncoa.org

~

Eldercare Locator, a public service of the United States Administration on Aging connecting you with services for older adults and their families. See,

http://www.eldercare.gov/Eldercare.NET/Public/Index.aspx

~

PBS's Caring for Your Parents – A Caregiver's Handbook: A free guide specifically designed to help you navigate the complexities of eldercare information and services. See,

http://www.pbs.org/wgbh/caringforyourparents/handbook/gettingstarted/

~

Caregiving Planning Guide for Families - Create a caregiving plan with this helpful guide. It was developed by AARP to help make the job more manageable. It includes information on how to have vital conversations with older family members, organize important documents, assess your loved one's needs and locate important resources.

http://www.aarp.org/home-family/caregiving/info-07-2012/prepare-to-care-planning-guide.html?intcmp=AE-CRC-PLAN-BASIC-SPOT2

Epilogue

GREED IS A WORD FOR the extreme, grasping, devouring, degenerative, antisocial behavior that destroys families – a gluttonous, insatiable desire for money, power and tangible things. It is often the obliteration of the family unit and the ones we purportedly love. It is offering a smile and warm words on one hand while grasping her last dollar with the other, perhaps wrongfully endorsing her monthly Social Security check.

My best advice is 'do not simply wallow in self-pity,' take action to recoup your assets, and allow justice to take its course. After all, we are dealing with thieves – I no longer consider them family, and thieves deserve punishment.

Better yet, prevent the abuse – employ the safe guards I have suggested and do not succumb to incessant pleas for financial assistance. Help then, if necessary by educating them to fend for themselves. Remember you are not a bank in the business of lending money – even to family. The probability of repayment is nil.

I am not suggesting that you should not make financial gifts to family members. Many of us do that from time to time. There is a considerable difference between a voluntary gift of money or property to a family member, and being the victim of a financial scam or theft by a family member. If you are a senior living alone, seek assistance of your attorney, clergy, local police department senior liaison, or close friend. This is not the time for action by you alone!

Finally, when in doubt – when circumstances seem suspect – simply do not do it. You will need those funds in your retirement.

<u>Remember</u>: *The faster you can signal for rescue, the faster you get out of that situation.* Joseph Teti

Made in the USA
Middletown, DE
06 March 2020